Writing and coloring book

Name:......................
Class:........................

Writing practise Number 1-10

Letters A-Z & Coloring

Coloring

Letters A-D

* **write and say.**

Avocado

Bicycle

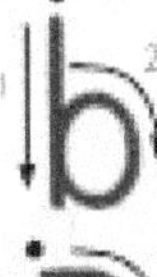

Cat

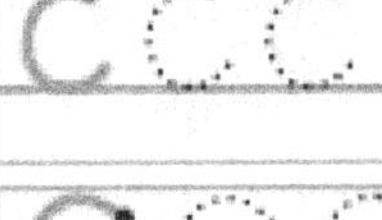

Coloring

Writing

Aa Bb Cc Dd

AA

a a

BB

b b

CC

c c

DD

d d

Avocado

Bicycle

Cat

Dog

Coloring

Letters E-H

* **write and say.**

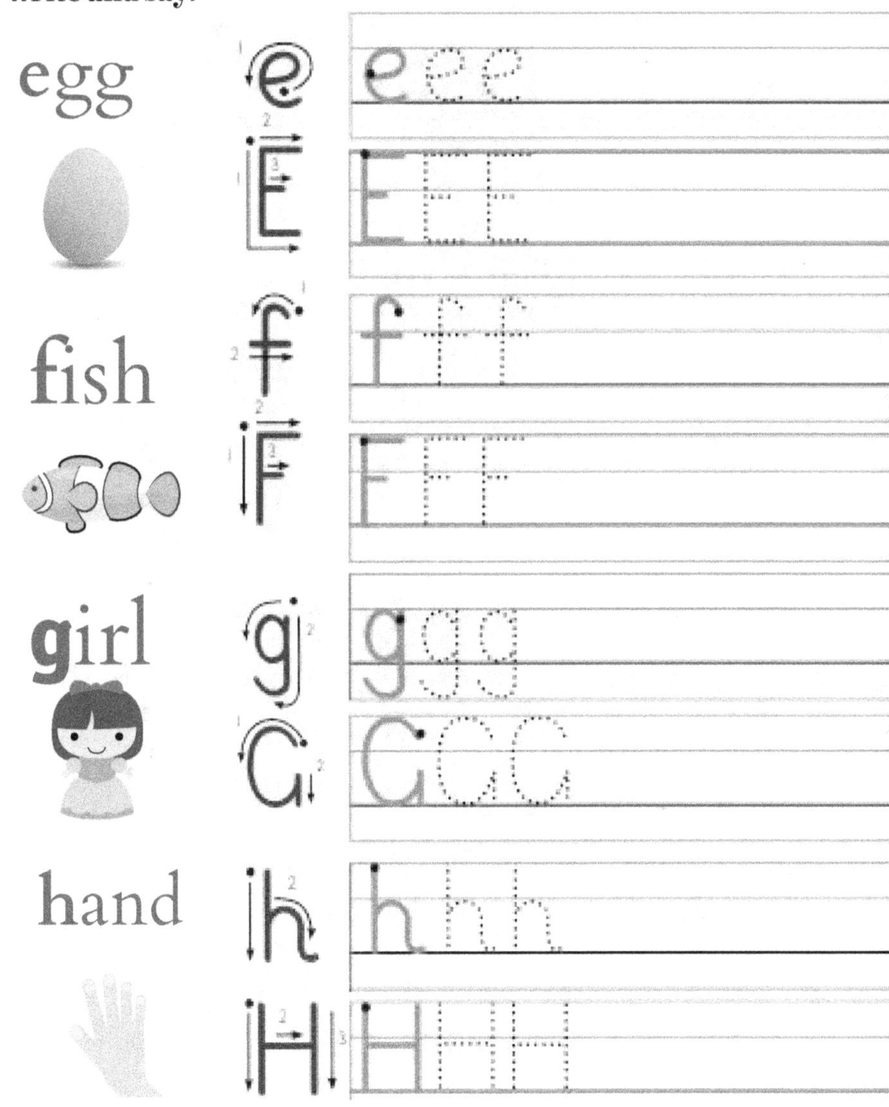

Coloring

Writing

Ee Ff Gg Hh

E E

e e

F F

f f

G G

g g

H H

h h

Egg

Fish

Girl

Hand

Coloring

Letters I-L

* **write and say.**

insect

jug

koala

Lemon

Coloring

Writing

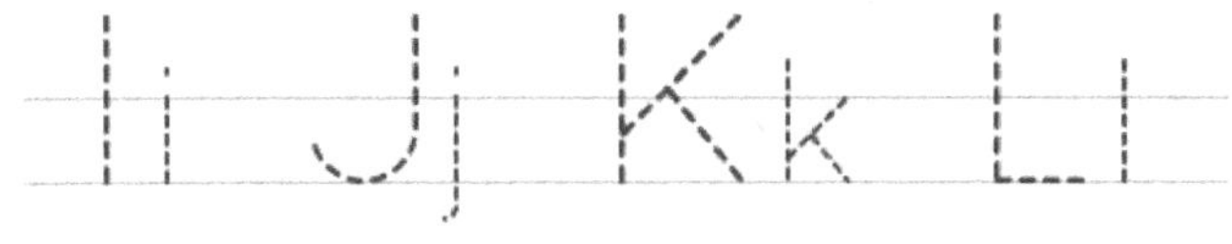

I I

i i

J J

j j

K K

k k

L L

l l

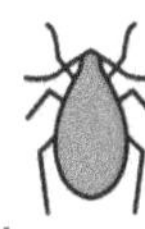

Insect

Jug

Koala

Lemon

Coloring

Letters M-P

* write and say.

Man

m m m m

M M M M

Night

n n n n

N N N N

Oal

o o o o

O O O O

Pen

p p p p

P P P P

Coloring

Writing

Mm Nn Oo Pp

MM

mm

NN

n n

OO

o o

P P

p p

Man

Night

Oal

Pen

Coloring

Letters Q-T

* **write and say.**

Queen

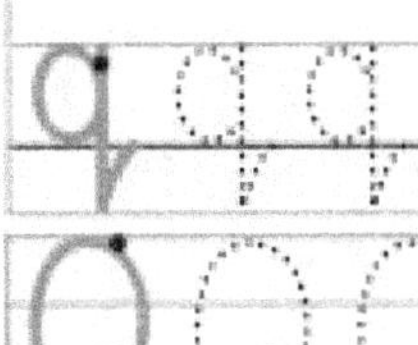

Rainbow

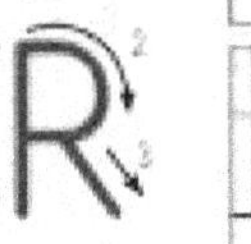

Sun

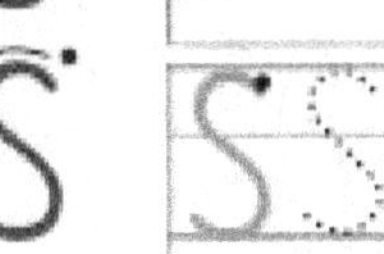

Taxi

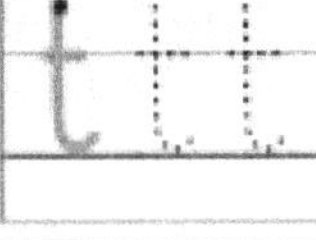

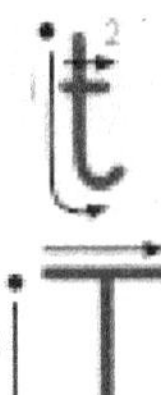

Coloring

Writing

Qq Rr Ss Tt

Q Q

q q

R R

r r

S S

s s

T T

t t

Queen

Rainbow

Sun

Taxi

Coloring

Letters U-X

* **write and say.**

Unicorn

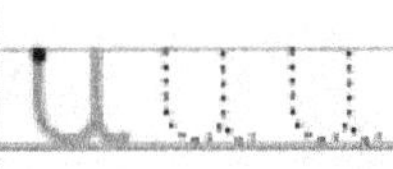

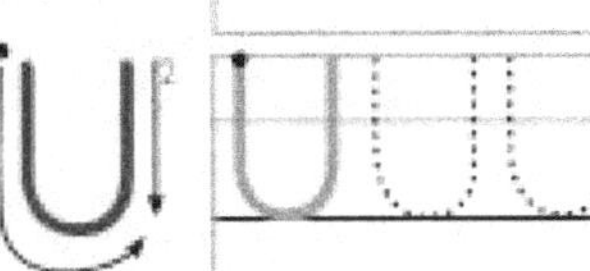

Volley-ball

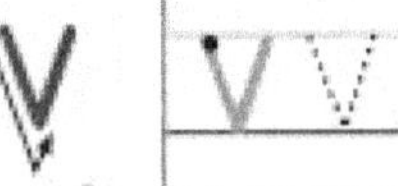

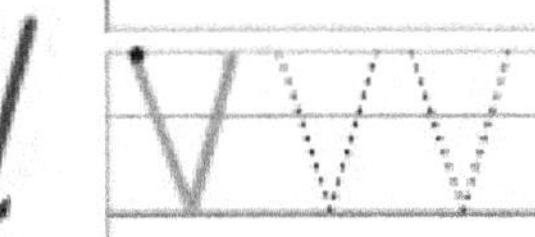

Wolf

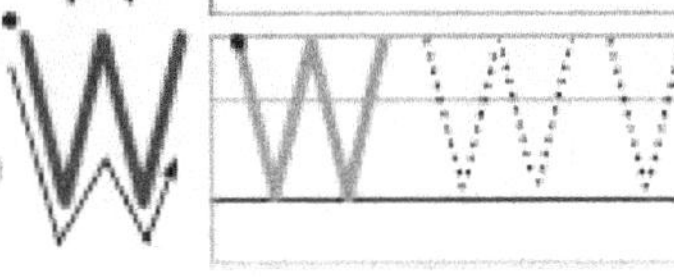

BOX

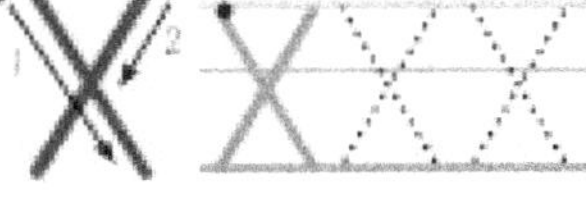

Coloring

Writing

U U

u u

V V

v v

W W

w w

X X

x x

Unicorn

Volley-ball

Wolf

BOX

Coloring

Letters Y-Z

* **write and say.**

Yoyo y y y y

Y Y Y Y

Zebra z z z z

Z Z Z Z

Y Y

y y

Z Z

z z

Coloring

Write All Words

Zebra

Wolf

Hand

Fish

Girl

Box

Unicorn

Violin

Sun

Taxi

Rabbit

Coloring

Writing Numbers

1 1 1 1

2 2 2 2

3 3 3 3

4 4 4 4

5 5 5 5

6 6 6 6

7 7 7 7

8 8 8 8

9 9 9 9

10 10 10 10

Coloring

Coloring Numbers

1 2 3 4

5 6 7 8

9 10

Coloring

Coloring

Coloring

Coloring

Coloring

Coloring

5

5

5

Coloring

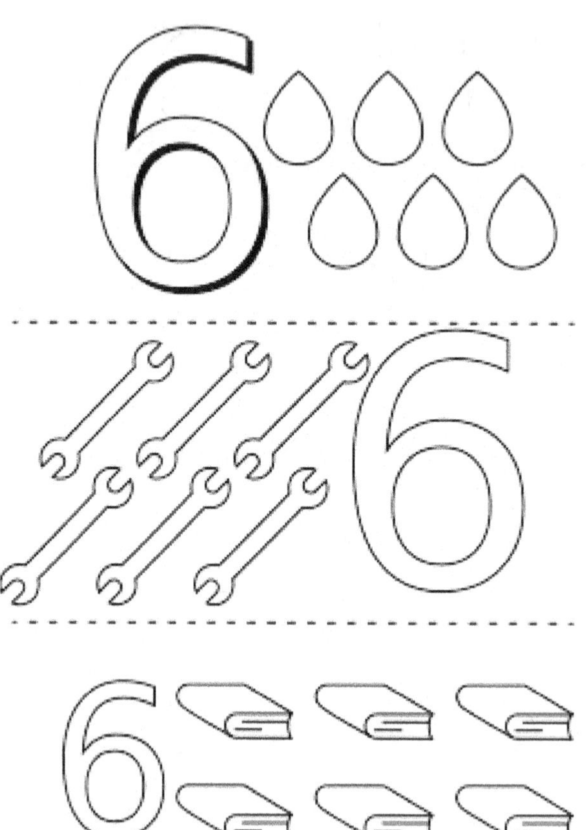

Coloring

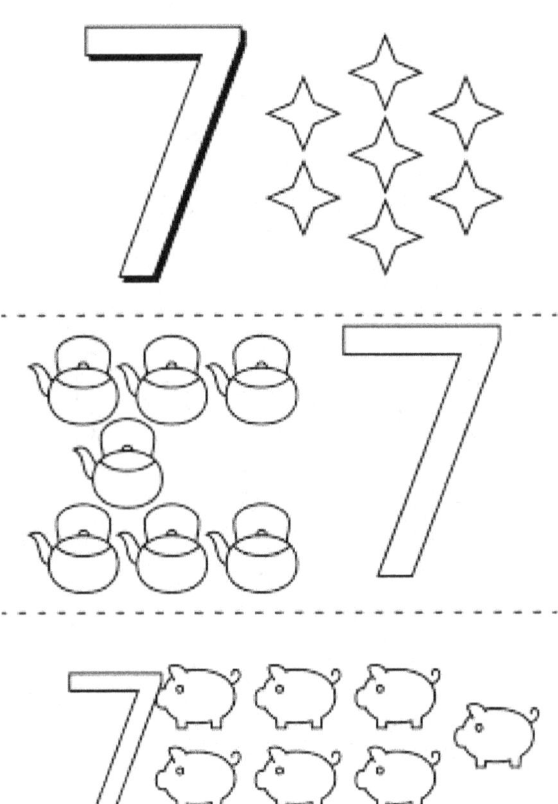

Coloring

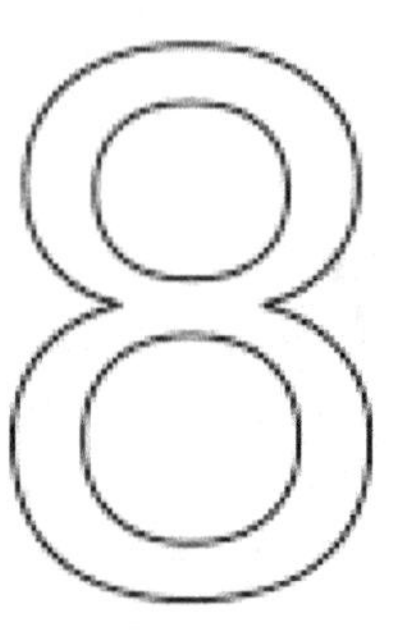

Coloring

Coloring

www.ingramcontent.com/pod-product-compliance
Lightning Source LLC
Chambersburg PA
CBHW071039260726
48661CB00007B/3069
* 9 7 9 8 6 6 3 5 9 5 9 2 6 *